The Patron Saints of Knitting

Poems by

Nancy Keating

Finishing Line Press
Georgetown, Kentucky

The Patron Saints of Knitting

Copyright © 2022 by Nancy Keating
ISBN 978-1-64662-785-1 First Edition
All rights reserved under International and Pan-American Copyright Conventions. No part of this book may be reproduced in any manner whatsoever without written permission from the publisher, except in the case of brief quotations embodied in critical articles and reviews.

ACKNOWLEDGMENTS

The author is grateful to these publications, which accepted the following works:

New Letters: "Prayer to Saint Isidore, Patron Saint of Animal Husbandry," "Prayer to Saint Mark, Patron Saint of Lawyers and Notaries" (also reprinted by *Poetry Daily*), "Prayer to Saint Meridel, Matron Saint of Lefties," "Prayer to Sister Magpie, Matron Saint of Materials"

The Southampton Review: "Prayer to Saint Acrylius, Patron Saint of Synthetics," "Prayer to Saint Dita Von Graph, Matron Saint of Measurement," "Prayer to Saint Lydia, Patroness of Dyers," "Prayer to Saint Maureen, Matron Saint of Irish Knitters"

Publisher: Leah Huete de Maines
Editor: Christen Kincaid
Cover Art: Shawn Uttendorfer
Author Photo: Lonna Sullivan, Smile Bella Photo
Cover Design: Elizabeth Maines McCleavy

Order online: www.finishinglinepress.com
also available on amazon.com

Author inquiries and mail orders:
Finishing Line Press
P.O. Box 1626
Georgetown, Kentucky 40324
USA

Table of Contents

Prayer to Sister Magpie, Matron Saint of Materials 1

Prayer to Saint Acrylius, Patron Saint of Synthetics 2

Prayer to Saint Dita Von Graph, Matron Saint of Measurement ... 3

Prayer to Saint Norah, Head Matron Saint of Knitting
and All Its Tools and Gear 4

Prayer to Saint Spangle, Matron Saint of Embellishments.............. 5

Prayer to Sir Thomas More, Patron Saint of Politicians 6

Prayer to Saint Joseph, Patron Saint of Cabinetmakers................... 7

Prayer to Saint Clare, Matron Saint of Projects 8

Prayer to Saint Isidore, Patron Saint of Animal Husbandry........... 9

Prayer to Saint Martin of Tours, Patron Saint of Pacifists............. 10

Prayer to Saint Melania, Patroness of Trophy Wives 11

Prayer to Saint Judas, Patron Saint of Betrayal............................... 12

Prayer to Saint Billiejean, Matron Saint of Muscle Memory 13

Prayer to Blessed Sister Brad, Patron of Implements..................... 14

Prayer to Saint Meridel, Matron Saint of Lefties 15

Prayer to Saint Maureen, Matron Saint of Irish Knitters 16

Prayer to Saint Reversaline, Matron Saint of the Do-Over........... 17

Prayer to Saint Mark, Patron Saint of Lawyers and Notaries........ 18

Prayer to Saint Symbolica, Matron Saint of Patterns..................... 19

Prayer to Saint Jude, Patron Saint of Futility 20

Prayer to Saint Lydia, Patroness of Dyers.. 21

The web of our life is of a mingled yarn, good and ill together.

—*William Shakespeare*

Prayer to Sister Magpie
Matron Saint of Materials

Dear Sister Magpie, whatever I can cast on or wind up, help me make of it a thing of funky originality. Let not any scarcities of conventional yarn stop me. Grant me the vision to see what can become of old cassette tape, the odd shoelace, the bits of ribbon saved from Christmas presents, my grandmother's frugal ball of recycled string, the plastic bags ripped into strips, fishing line, dental floss, gardening twine, and even spools of electrical cable. Oh Matron Saint of Materials, bestow on me also the gift of time so that I may knit 24-7 in a parallel life even as I satisfy the demands of others on me, and grant that I may never do violence to another using tensile piano wire, but instead knit it up into a small kitchen appliance or something similar.
Amen.

Prayer to Saint Acrylius
Patron Saint of Synthetics

Oh beloved Saint Acrylius, you who was favored by Woolworth's and Newberry's and Lee Ward and so many five-and-dimes of yore, please shine your light on my request to God for forgiveness for my long-ago sin of making and giving all my friends those knitted (but mainly crocheted) vests and headbands and bags and whatever else might be trimmed with fringe or macramé in those dreadful DayGlo back-to-the-earth colors so current back then, so humiliating now, looking through these fading orange Polaroids—although, to be fair, Saint, when one is young and lovely no stratosphere of tackiness in wardrobe can truly succeed in making your radiant health ridiculous. My old friends grin and glow, shoulder to shoulder, so high and happy in their Seventies orangey-gold-avocado acrylic granny-square vests, with their muttonchops and Afros and ironed Peggy Lipton curtain of hair. Those nasty vests, so pilled and matted, would outlive us unless one were to be torched by the spark of an errant reefer. So many of us, in our marijuana hazes and our literature seminars, smiled like sunsets back then, Saint. Some are no longer with us, Acrylius. If you see them, apologize for me, and say I knew not what I was doing.
Amen.

Prayer to Saint Dita Von Graph
Matron Saint of Measurement

Oh Blessed Saint Dita, your shape stays in your memory, your body is your yardstick, and your wingspan equals your height. Dearly beloved Matron Saint of Measurement, bless us with the understanding of rules of thumb, such that a foot measured shall forever be a foot, as is the elbow to wrist, and help us conjure even from the legally-mandated 100-yard distance the proper measurements of the former lovers we stalk, that we may continue to knit them unwanted yet beautiful sweaters and vests, despite the fact that all this devotion freaked said ex-lovers out and they called us clingy and codependent and they didn't want to commit themselves to a relationship right now. Grant that the famous knitting curse be lifted and that these same ungrateful yet deeply hot former lovers come to see the error of their ways and return to our woolly embrace. In you, Saint Dita, we place our trust. Amen.

Prayer to Saint Norah
Head Matron Saint of Knitting and All Its Tools and Gear

Oh talented Saint Norah, from whom such beautiful garments come, bless my pattern book, that I may select and understand the pattern that best suits my humble knowledge of knitting. As you know, Saint, I'm not much for the domestic arts, but I'd much rather knit than cook—cooking can get so squishy or splattery, a lot like children, but knitting is dry. I don't mind being dry, at last. Bless this yarn, of course, the *sine qua non*, the fuse that detonates, the sin that commits. Bless my needles, these humdrum pointy sticks, that I may disrupt the conventional wisdom of the poncho. Bless my cable needle, that two-edged tool I use to twist the stitches here, and again there and there, into pleasantly demented surfaces. Bless these humble markers, tiny rubbery rings that slip on the needle to separate stitches and show me where I am. It's always important to know where we are, I find, don't you, Saint? And bless these bobbins, that they may keep the colors of yarn not currently in use safely nearby and tangle-free. Bless the row-counter, that I may remember to advance the little clicker on it so that each row counts. That's funny, isn't it, Saint? of course every row counts—play on words. Okay, it's not all that funny. Now if you would, please give me a special blessing for my tape measure, that I may cease to knit one sleeve longer than the other two. Wait. Oh dear. While you're at it, Saint, please bless my stitch holders, those absurd jumbo safety pins, with which I hold raw stitches at the neck of the sweater back while working wicked fast on the front part coming up to meet it, and can connect back to front while finishing the neck. What's that, Saint? Which word did you object to—was it "coming"? "wicked"? Oh. "Sin." All right, bless this project bag, that I may keep all tools for one project aside from the rest and safe from disaster until you forgive me for whatever. Right.
Amen.

Prayer to Saint Spangle
Matron Saint of Embellishments

Dearly beloved Saint Spangle, you of the sequins and baubles, the feathers and pompoms, give us the imagination to see what small household objects might be incorporated into these drab offerings we create for our loved ones, especially my friend Alice, who is allergic to wool and only wears understated colors. Grant us the persistence required to thread the pearls and beads, all 700 of them, onto the boring cotton yarn I must use to quickly make Alice a scarf, yet another goddamned scarf, excuse my blasphemy, for her birthday which is right around the corner. Through your intercession with Jesus, who both you and Alice are on better terms with than I am, guide me as I make Alice something beautiful and fun, that Alice may wear it and rejoice during one of her innumerable daily visits to her fragile 94-year-old mother, who has tired of living but can't let herself die and may drag Alice down with her. Dear Saint Spangle, I praise your love of flashiness. Together may we channel that love into a happy accessory.
Amen.

Prayer to Sir Thomas More
Patron Saint of Politicians

Your Grace, you may find this an odd request, but my knitting guild really needs guidance. It's been hijacked by a new president, and you would not believe the palace intrigues and pot-stirring we've got. Once upon a time, Sir Tom,—may I call you that?—our guild was a utopian place where women sat peaceably and knitted and chatted and did all the things the haters laughed at us for and not always behind our backs, but we were happy. We organized bus trips to alpaca farms. We made chemo caps for cancer patients and hats for the veterans. Then our longtime president, who had some family issues, decided not to run for another term. Donna raised her hand and volunteered, so she was elected. She held it together till May, and then she brought the crazy, telling Group A that Group B looked down on them, accusing half the board of being against her in an email that went to the whole membership. Sir Tom, ours is a small empire, but she's got a two-year term. People are skipping meetings. People say they're quitting. Execution isn't an option, sadly. We're thinking of a coup. We're looking for a loophole. What do we do? What would you do?
Amen.

Prayer to Saint Joseph
Patron Saint of Cabinetmakers

Saint Joseph, stepfather to Jesus, who raised Him to succeed you in a carpenter's trade, you glow in the window at Chartres, both you and the boy, smoothing a slab of cedar. Please bless my cabinets and trunks and crates, the built-ins that came with the house along with the bureau my neighbor set out at the curb and which I dragged across the street to take possession of in my never-ending quest for storage for my handknits. For while my balls of yarn can remain in their totebags or even rest temporarily, a couple of years at the max, in stackable plastic storage bins, what I make deserves to live in wood. Wood that's planed and drawers that are dovetailed. In butternut, maple and pine. Saint, it's the least they deserve, my bulky demonstrations of love. Some of us keep everything. Look here: I have an old boyfriend who's saved the sweater I made him in college, a grey one with cables. I know because he sent me a picture of it, posed on a hanger, matted in plexiglass. He had someone sew elbow patches onto it, his wife, I expect. So there it was, an elephant in the middle of somebody else's marriage. Saint Joseph, please inspire him to give it a drawer, and a rest after all this time hanging.
Amen.

Prayer to Saint Clare
Matron Saint of Projects

Oh Saint Clare of Assisi, you who have forsaken your noble family, as did Saint Francis, to establish an order of nuns and an abbey in the hills above town alongside Saint Francis—and we'll gloss over our questions about that alliance—look favorably on me who confidently has recourse to your intercession with Jesus. Oh sister of sackcloth and simple brown and black garments, guide my choices from among my hundreds of printed and online knitting projects, that I may select only those which should most fittingly become a completed one. Help me reduce my ungainly hoarder stash of yarn to a tasteful minimalism. Oh you who lived in a cave, hear my prayer and bless my patterns, that when completed they might demonstrate the same tasteful simplicity one finds in the humble ateliers of Florence. Deliver me from the slings of verbal abuse and catcalls from those who find my completed work sloppy and amateurish, and give me the grace to refrain from laughing at these idiots who do not recognize handmade craftsmanship when they see it. Hear, Saint Clare, my constant prayer.
Amen.

Prayer to Saint Isidore
Patron Saint of Animal Husbandry

Oh Saint Isidore, through whose care and dedication we fiber addicts find it possible to score handspun natural undyed yarn at the farmers' market on Saturdays, please grant a long and virile life to Richie, the black ram whose nappy patch of fleece I scratched last Tuesday while visiting a sheep farm upstate. Richie and I had a moment, Saint, him with his wide intelligent hazel eyes, regarding me across the chasm of unrelated mammals. He ate the grass I offered; he ate the grass in his pen. It was all the same to him. Like you, he does his part, Saint. You roll up your sleeves and muck out the pens, while like a biblical prophet, he knows 40 ewes a year. Patiently he offers up his curly coat to the carder, the spinner, the knitter, the factories of the world, asking nothing more than a field of grass and the occasional rub between his horns. As grows the fleece, so spins the yarn. Black sheep, black roving, black yarn, textured when spun by hand, with traces of lanolin inherent. Pray God for long life to Richie the Wise, and blessings on all his kin.
Amen.

Prayer to Saint Martin of Tours
Patron Saint of Pacifists

Oh humble Saint Martin, you who embody the spirit of pretty much all Christ's beatitudes, I pray to you today with a heavy heart. Dear Saint, I'm fully aware—who isn't?—that we live in violent times, but I'm wondering how you feel, as a retired military man yourself, about yarn bombing. This is the strange practice whereby yarn in gaudy and clashing colors is employed to knit blatantly homemade-looking sleeves for such ugly aspects of our human landscape as utility poles, bike racks, traffic signals, even sometimes the trunks of trees. To achieve this objective, teams of women must meet at zero-dark-thirty to position and stitch their creations to the hardscape to be thusly adorned. Saint, I've been told that a cop once interrupted a yarn-bombing maneuver, and was so perplexed by this weird form of vandalism that he could only send the ladies home with some kind of warning, perhaps along the lines of "don't make a public excrescence any worse." Just my opinion, Saint. I need enlightenment, and I hope you can provide it; do these so-called bomb squads suffer from a lack of danger in their lives? Is it admirable to adopt the language of terrorists and crazies to justify this particular use for leftover yarn? Excuse me for shouting. Please help me knit in peace.
Amen.

Prayer to Saint Melania
Patroness of Trophy Wives

Oh glamorous Melania, you of the slashing cheekbones and smoldering eyes, while you may not be canonized yet—for that one needs to be dead, actually—I thank you for your contributions to the heightened renown of knitting, though I know it was far from intentional. I read in the *Times* where you knitted navy-blue sweaters, more than one, as a young girl in little Sevnica, your charming Slovenian nowheresville of fewer than five thousand souls. You and your girlfriends passed notes between houses on strings of yarn, notes about the boys you might marry or love and what the webs to ensnare them might be. The article mentioned navy-blue sweaters, plural, always navy blue, and I wondered what was up with that, Melania. Maybe it was to go with your uniform for school. I had a navy one, too. In Google's photo gallery, every picture shows you posing in solid colors. Sleek. You started early, I guess. After you gave that speech you cribbed from Michelle, the white dress you were wearing sold out. You favor white dresses, I see—kind of like a uniform for a bride. I always like to see what we find noteworthy and what is passed over. Me, I think of a sweater as the starting of something, an entire garment built out of a single thread. In a way, we make ourselves. Melania, show us your navy-blue sweaters, your building blocks. We need something to aspire to, that won't unravel, these days especially.
Amen.

Prayer to Saint Judas
Patron Saint of Betrayal

Saint Judas, you who made your name by selling out the One dearest to you, help me find the words to ask God for forgiveness in the area of handicraft. When thirty pieces of silver is the cost of a handknit scarf from Macy's, and also the going rate for one hank of hand-painted fingering yarn, you'd be the first to understand why I'm tempted to make the fast grab for flashy style sometimes, rather than the slow, methodical, occasionally tedious yet mostly-always satisfying reward of creating a scarf that's reserved only to me. And yet, as I'm sure you'll testify, it's not easy to stick to your principles all the time, and sometimes you can slip and get back on track before anybody notices. Obviously Jesus does, but He forgives everything. I still haven't decided if that's unstinting love or just idiocy. Recall that when the Roman soldiers divided up the robes of Jesus for themselves, they tore His cloak by the seams—and that's pretty cold but at least it's recycling, sort of—but they had to cast lots for His tunic. Why is that? Theologians think His tunic was knit in one piece on circular needles. Saint, theologians have a lot of time to waste, don't they? Personally, I'd kill myself. (Sorry, figure of speech.)
Amen.

Prayer to Saint Billiejean
Matron Saint of Muscle Memory

Praise to you, Saint Billiejean, and buzz and hosannas! It's you we think of when our hands, arms and fingers move to the clack of our tools, naturally, as coordinated as a knitting machine, smooth and automatic. Give thanks with us, Saint, to the Creator who made us with the gift of autonomic nerves. Thanks to Her we talk and knit, we read and knit, we visit and think, always applying the front of our brain to the obvious task while that same amazing computer runs our hands, working in the background. Call it mechanical. Call it multitasking. When I was 12, I taught myself how as a party trick. People are astounded to see me do it, out-and-out gobsmacked, I tell you. Why would that be, Saint Billiejean? If a man can walk and chew gum at once, why can't a woman knit while running the world? Silly question. Of course we can, although personally I draw the line at twisting cables when reading *The New York Times*. I've seen pictures of Shetland Island fishwives knitting as they walked along the shore, their yarn in their aprons. That's because there was money in their output. You know how that goes; give us incentive and we can adapt.
Amen.

Prayer to Blessed Sister Brad
Patron of Implements

Oh Blessed Sister Brad, straight as an arrow, in you we place our confidence. Grant us the talent to knit even and regular rows regardless of whatever long pointy tools we may be reduced to using due to our regular needles already being tied up in other projects that lie about our house unfinished in a pile on our side of the living-room sofa and our side of the bed. Spare us the golf clubs but give us the shish-kebab skewers, spokes from dead umbrellas, three-inch nails, and cake testers, all of which we know that, with your intercession, can be repurposed in the interests of divine creativity, that gift from God. We know you're not a saint yet, but like ourselves, you are a work in progress; help us pull off a miracle or two, that we may ease your path to canonization. Prayer works both ways.
Amen.

Prayer to Saint Meridel
Matron Saint of Lefties

Oh, radical Saint Meridel, you who told the interviewer that victimhood made all women fearful, and who admitted you were always intimidated and afraid, the beauty is that no one could tell from your books. Help me face and overcome the dread. For I do have dread, and have been a victim, a word I disdain. Saint, I have tried to live life with my head down, but even in knitting, my differences show. My cables twist left instead of right. When I follow a pattern precisely, the buttonholes wind up on the men's side. I don't want to be a man; I just covet their birthright. I find security in knitting circles, safe places where no man deigns to enter. Short of more self-defense classes, we all know the rules: backs to the wall, knives out. In our case, needles and scissors. Saint Meridel, you who lost your house because the FBI suspected your leanings and their watchfulness kept driving lodgers away, console me in my anxiety, which sits deep inside me and ranges over many subjects, physical to financial. At 3 a.m. I lie awake under my mother's afghan, restless with the common womanly terror of finding herself alone in an unfamiliar meadow, no one knowing where she is, concerned that some stranger might happen along. Oh Saint, let me not show weakness. Help me throw out the rulebook.
Amen.

Prayer to Saint Maureen
Matron Saint of Irish Knitters

Say it ain't so, Saint Moe! (May I call you Moe? that's what we call my Aunt Maureen…) I've been reading secular books that say the Aran Isle sweater was the creation of some branch of the Irish tourist board. Skewer my Celtic pride! Growing up in the blandest and flattest of suburbs and the newest of houses, still I was an Irish lass, complete with the requisite freckles and naturally-curly hair. And tribal forces conspired to bring the Clancy Brothers albums into the house, each showcasing a row of men in their cream-colored pullovers. All Erin all the time. Saint Moe, I spent school afternoons learning to knit while Mom and I sang along to "The Whistling Gypsy" and "Four Green Fields." Half my schoolmates had Irish names. When the nuns got new habits, we thrilled to see Sister Franny X was a redhead. We taught each other jigs and reels in the playground—if nobody brought the jump-rope. And now I find the Clancys were nothing more than stage Irishmen whose agent bought their wardrobes. My ethnic faith is shaken to the core. Next you'll tell me the Irish eat their young. No, wait—that was an ex-friend of my parents', and she was speaking for herself, the way hers turned out. Pardon me. Pardon me all to hell. Amen.

Prayer to Saint Reversaline
Matron Saint of the Do-Over

Oh patient Saint Reversaline, I need to tell you, you are the knitting saint I find most difficult to pray to. Yet, I believe you alone would understand my dilemma. I just ripped out an entire boatneck sweater, right up to the neck, because that's where the problem started with this thing. Call it original sin. People who pray, and even the rest of us, know all about original sin, the idea that you don't even start out perfect, and then it's all downhill from there. So if that's the case, why should anyone even try to do things well? The yarn only cost me $20. I could get online and order myself a cotton striped boatneck pullover that channels Audrey Hepburn at her most appealing, with that swanlike neck she had. (My mother used to envy my swanlike neck. She is gone. No one else ever took note of my neck.) But no. In fact, I can't do that, can't bring myself to put a bad sweater in the trash. It's not the sweater's fault I put the front and back next to each other and both sleeves on the same side. It's me. I was too hasty. I saw the sweater completed and lovely, and failed to embrace the process. Saint, if you would, guide me to that zen state other people assume I get from these string and sticks. Amen.

Prayer to Saint Mark
Patron Saint of Lawyers and Notaries

Gracious Saint Mark, evangelist, apostle, and all-around good writer, you who are patron saint of lawyers, notaries, and prisoners—so, basically, the designated protector of those who labor under the constraints of bureaucracy—grant me the patience to sit through the interminable hearings orchestrated by my local municipality to bore the public to death so that, after most people go home to bed, the zoning board may move in favor of the big property owner. Saint Mark, keep me mindful that I, alone in the room, was the only person apart from the developer to accomplish anything, in his case approval of a $20 million deal, in my case half of a glowing gold mohair shawl in the feather-and-fan pattern. (Although, to be fair, that's an excellent suit the council president is wearing, beautifully cut.) I understand that as patron of paper-pushers, you and I might be at cross-purposes, but you are also the patron saint of lions, and who knew magisterial tawny lions prayed? As a civic watchdog, I try to embody the saying, "They also serve who only sit and wait." Who said that, Saint, and were they serious? Please tell me which side you're on.
Amen.

Prayer to Saint Symbolica
Matron Saint of Patterns

Saint Symbolica, this is my angry prayer. Could you please watch over the Norahs and Marys and Debbies, the knitting design gurus of the world—sorry for the non-Catholic term, but that's what they are, avatars of originality—and guide their hands and brains and graph-paper notations so that they do not pass along their screwups to us. Debbie is the worst, Saint. We put our faith in these designers, we flock to their workshops, we follow them like fangirls, and in return sometimes they waste our time for us, with their erroneous stitch counts and abbreviations, equating pass-slipped-stitch-over with yarn-over-twice—two completely different things, Saint Symbolica. I'm fully aware that copying the work of the masters, or mistresses, if you will, keeps me a slave to imitation, but in any art form, copying leads to mastery. Mistressy? But I have reached maturity, Saint, so they'd better not push me. I don't have time to make nice little sweaters. They say it's a sign of humility to put an error into your work, so you're not showing God up with your expertise. I can twist a cable with the best of them but trust me, there's no danger of perfection in anything I do.
Amen.

Prayer to Saint Jude
Patron Saint of Futility

Oh, persevering Saint Jude, you're kind of a staple in the pantheon but I've never understood why people pray to you. Do you actually act to achieve any kind of concrete result, or do the prayers only make people feel better? You're a little bit existential, a little bit pointless. Okay then, here I am with a prayer of my own. Please find some meaning for a knitter who continues to knit with wool yarn in the face of global warming. Winter gets shorter and shorter; my stack of sweaters grows ever higher. I have a worthless skill. Higher temperatures strip warm sweaters of their value, while rising floodwaters saturate the fibers and drag their wearers down. If a machine did what I do, they'd sell it for scrap. Yet I continue to knit. Cotton yarn has no give. Silk yarn sort of flops like a dead fish. Linen fiber costs too much. I'm a hopeless case. Should you take away my needles? Help me. Give me a higher purpose. Not that I care about a higher purpose. Do what you can, Saint. Or else just lock me up; there I'll be in the yarn room, rocking forward and back, counting stitches to myself in monotone. At least I'd be happy in my little trance.
Amen.

Prayer to Saint Lydia
Patroness of Dyers

Oh alchemical Saint Lydia, first-century stirrer of cauldrons of flowers and leaves, give us this day the orange fiber from the skin of red onions, the miracle of indigo, the tawny earth of walnut husks, and please refrain from reminding us that sometimes the truest shades can wash out and fade like a memory. Saint Lydia, you know first-hand what can come of the lowliest weed. I'm thinking about the happiest yellow of any field of dandelions, our yard, the yellow ink they made on a playsuit I had then. I lay on my stomach among them, this field of gold, like coins, like the pet canary my father named after a Swedish tenor, among the bees, air-hanging and dusted with pollen. And that was the end of the playsuit, the stains no mother or miracle-working detergent could remove, stains like a rapturous sin. Now I boil the blossoms and brew an amber tea, then scoop out the flowers and throw in the hanks of wool. Then stir. Then steep. Then drain and rinse and there it is again, the yellow of morning in June. Saint, I want to make love to the yellow, eat it and drink it and bathe in it. Yet all I have in my hand, really, is three hanks of yarn. It's like the potential for love, Saint, or genius. We dream it into our reach. Then we awake and it fades like a color in the sun. Saint, we need it back.
Amen.

Nancy Keating has been knitting and writing poetry for most of her life, but has not always treated either of these pursuits seriously. She remembers knitting a whole sweater at age ten because her classmate Maria had beaten her to it and wore hers to school. Nancy kept knitting throughout high school and college, knitted a few sweaters for boyfriends who promptly broke up with her, and then put her needles on hiatus for a couple of decades.

This series of poems grew out of a writers' workshop where participants were instructed to write three prayers to imaginary gods, like those in Ovid's *Metamorphoses*. She made the decision to draw on her Catholic upbringing; after finding no patron saints of knitting, invented a few of her own; and continued writing "prayers" past the original three because she found it a flexible format in which to explore ideas about love, memory, mortality, and even contemporary life. Plus, she was having fun with it.

Retired from a career in communications and marketing, Nancy earned a second master's degree—an MFA in creative writing from Stony Brook University—and currently teaches in the English department at Farmingdale State College. Her second book of poems, *White Chick* (2021), won the Antivenom Award from Elixir Press. Her work has appeared in *New Letters, Gettysburg Review, New American Writing, The Southampton Review, Carolina Quarterly, Southwest Review,* and elsewhere, as well as online in *Poetry Daily* and *American Life in Poetry*.

www.ingramcontent.com/pod-product-compliance
Lightning Source LLC
LaVergne TN
LVHW041522070426
835507LV00012B/1764